Apostrophes V

Never Born Except Within the Other

Apostrophes V

Never Born Except Within the Other

E.D. Blodgett

BuschekBooks

National Library of Canada Cataloguing in Publication

Blodgett, E. D. (Edward Dickinson), 1935-
       Apostrophes V : never born except within the other / E.D. Blodgett.

Poems.
ISBN 1-894543-13-0

       I. Title. II. Title: Apostrophes five. III. Title: Apostrophes 5.

PS8553.L56A765 2003   C811'.54   C2003-902015-0
PR9199.3.B54A92 2003

Cover Design by JulieAnne Muth

This book is set in AGaramond and Baker Signet.

Printed in Canada by Hignell Book Printing, Winnipeg, Manitoba.

BuschekBooks gratefully acknowledges the support of the Canada Council for the Arts and the
Ontario Arts Council for its publishing program.

BuschekBooks
P.O. Box 74053, 5 Beechwood Avenue
Ottawa, Ontario K1M 2H9
Canada
Email: buschek.books@sympatico.ca

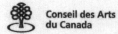 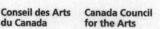 

jamais né sauf en l'autre

—Jacques Brault

Tibi

TABLE OF CONTENTS

FACE

Sometimes against the winter light your face becomes translucent, face
of parchment and an air in which millenia descend, and through
it frailties of trees come barely into sight, memories
of trees and birds that are the breath of winter light retreating, birds
that are of light and leaping from the dark into the dark, a light
against the trees uncertain—vespertudinal birds that disappear
into the twilight of your face. It is no face, it is the day
amorphous, branches of the trees floating upward through a sea

of light where snow is virtual, about to flower on the air.
Everything that is is tendency, neither here nor there,
a breath that enters us becoming momentarily our flesh,
or us asleep, lying side by side upon the hand of dark,
the only presence in the room our breathing that envelopes us
and rising through the window circulates among the wakefulness
of roses of a snow that is to be. We breathe the snow before
it is: it flowers on your face, and all the birds become fire.

STROPHES

The sacred dances. Nothing that we do it does not do. We sleep,
and it lies down to sleep in us. The trees around us sleep, and it
is the trees sleeping, air and leaf asleep, but sleep that is in each
of us a motion that is not of us, invisible anti-
strophe of what we are, appearance only of the dancing as
it takes momentary shape, each of us a turn that turns
in larger figures, ours through ours, a dance of many dances that

knows nothing but the turns it makes, and knows them never knowing where
they are or whose, a dance of dispossession that possesses when
its turn is taken. We are not able to be you or me, and when
it is that we are we, then we are of other shapes, of birds
that in their sudden leavings suddenly explode against the sun,
smaller planets indiscernible, the turning of the sun
all that they are, their passage us elsewhere, of sun and shade and air.

BEGINNINGS

In the beginning the sun opened, and whatever moons were in
the sky opened with the planets. Some were but stone, and some
were fire. So it was that stone and fire opened, standing in
the sky where they were placed. No other spring could be compared
to this, this opening of skies that are deeper than the seas
that we might gaze upon, of skies that open into further skies,
the blue that is above us open everywhere more intricate

than any flower. We open, the sky in us descending, suns
in their beginnings going forth. We are other flowers, the
invisible that seems to be the flesh we wear that rises, skies
our breath. We do not speak, but words are near us in the air. They turn
the way that suns turn, their inflections ours. Words are the last
to open: in them other skies and other flowers open in
their turn, words that speak our us in silence—fire, stone and spring.

CONSUMMATION

Before the words were found, we were not. It is not possible
to keep before our eyes the merest tree, the wind that moves among
its leaves, to see it in its consummation in the sun without
our knowing our being spoken at the end of things.
It is to be a seventh day within the speaking of the world,
a language everywhere around us to be carried, stones and blades
of grass, everything already said as it was to be said,
but not the grass in its simplicity, the green against our feet—

this is grass in consonance, its it a speaking, all that is
of its completion not within our eyes. This is our embrace,
to be another grass, our visibility within
the sun a silence that is of the stones, the trees. The we we are
is known as it is heard, as one might hear an epilogue, the rest
unsaid, but known as birds that pass around us in the dark, their cries
another light evoking suns in memory, their cries the leaves
of words that fall upon us from an autumn of eternities.

SNOW

Where we are, aspects of God are everywhere. They are not seen,
no more than dust upon a chair, its knowledge close upon our hands,
a knowledge that will never cross the mind, forgotten grass we walk
upon, but if it has the shape of thought, what is the thought that we
articulate, the we we say we are a syntax that unfolds
from our sleep and in its waking gazes on itself, a thing
of bone and flesh and light that makes an order of the world? We

do not think, but we are thought among its possibilities,
visions of the snow that take us by surprise, a snow about
to flower, breaths of air unsure, a space of snow invisible
between the words we speak, a silence big with birth upon our lips
that says us as it says whatever else might come to mind—the grass,
the dust or chair—and so we come to be in temporalities
of us and of whatever we are of, the snow in syllables.

KABBALAH

Think of God playing with the little stones, the stones becoming
alphabets, and universes slowly coming into sight
as anagrams, the sun a language of its own, its light upon
your face, a murmur in the dark of flesh conversing, filled with what
the sun might say, being composed of stones that speak in tongues, fires
of the Pentecost falling at random everywhere on us
and on the farthest planets, little stones of fire speaking of

our origin, of you and I in our flesh, uncertain near
the trees and grass, but you and I whose simplest words are not of our
possession, words that are an echo of the stones that God within
his fire cast upon the air before the air was anywhere,
a you and I that cannot know our merest sense, no more than we
can know what planets mean, possessing only kinship with the stones
that lie about us on the ground, their silence us in memory.

RETURNING

My father asked us all to stop and look, and so we stopped and saw
the sun and then the cloud and finally shadows of the rain that stood
upon horizons far from us. We were very young, and when
the light came over us, it was not light that we had known, and he
was sheathed in it, a light of rain and shade and solitudes of suns
receding in the afternoon. The trees were in the solitude,
and he, illumined from the west, did not reflect but seemed to be

the place where light that was more deeply filled with shade began to rise
into the air. That was the day that I beheld mortality,
and where you stood your body was invisible, and through it I
could see the sun and its finality, the rain that was not rain
but shade. Disappearance can be held, and then I held it, the
surprise and gravity of that possession falling through the rain
remembered, no one now between us and horizons of the day.

SHAPES

At that moment stones came into view and flowers caught the sun
that were before unseen, and now they stand with stones around, the same
as then, the sun and air exactly as they were when they rose up
into our eyes, spread out forever in the memory that we keep
of them that day when we were walking past and stopped to speak of them
surprised, the words we said grown thinner till they disappeared within
the light. The stones cannot be us, but they are of the figure that

we make, composing aspects of ourselves against the earth, when you
and I began becoming us, another child that stands upon
the children that we think we were beneath a separate sun, the words
we spoke a language not of us, and no more able than the stones
to hand us back and forth, hermetic childhoods whose silence is
a silence of the smallest flowers that were never seen but in
the sun that hovers over them and us they leap into our eyes

together, giving us ourselves, their shadows inexplicable
but near us when we stoop to see them losing shapes that had been theirs
upon the ground, their shadows now unseen in ours, the suns that made
them put aside and giving us ourselves within their shade, not wholly
us, but us as flower, stone and sun, their swift arrivals and
departures unforeseen, but harvested, a shape of us reborn
within the lengthened day our memory makes of us against the light.

ORPHEUS

You liked to touch trees, most of all birches standing in
their early landscapes, surprised to see themselves as trees, when they so soon
before possessed the shape of girls at play beside the quick streams of spring
but now a dance of sun and air in one place, the streams alone
disappearing in the distances unknown to birches: so
you were certain they could speak, and we would know their words if we
could hear, most of all their laughter spreading through the landscape that

they made, a landscape of a childhood that rose no longer in
your sight but came and went in fragments, centuries that were not yours,
places unknown to you, and all of it contained inside a sun
that when it passes over water bursts, the light going farther
into space until the memory within it is the guise
of memory, a shape of all that is recalled, invisible
against the sun, of laughter and its echoes—these are trees that you

would touch, their silence flowing over in your hands, and where it pools,
you are unable to withstand the coming back of spring, the dance
of childhoods that goes around inside your flesh, the memory
of birches poised to catch the fling of light before it goes, a dance
that radiates against a purer sun, the silence of the moves
they make sufficient music, transient and open song without
words, that once known is known forever, diaspora of trees

that are in one unalterable metamorphosis, of girls
that run beside the ancient streams, their arms translucent in the sun,
their voices far away, and had you heard them you would say that this
is how birches in their early landscapes speak, their movements in
the wind the words of their becoming trees, and trees that are the sun
in its unceasing distillations, all desire one desire,
to be a change of light and be it always, once remembered sun

that in its passage bears the dancing girls, the distant laughter, trees
and all desire upward, turning through the stars, to be the light
in its desire, there where birches are a primavera of
the mind, a landscape of the mind possessing its desire, no
unfolding, no beginnings, no finalities, the now, the one
now that is, and in your hands desire come to rest, the touch
of trees enough. They speak the sun, and you are fire speaking light.

ARIAS

The body that we are is ours but in time, possessing no
more of itself than that fragility of birds that comes and goes
into the seasons from which they sprang: and some return and some remain
in that place that they have ever sought, yet their fragility,
the air that passes through their wings surrounding them with emptiness,
is theirs, the immortality they have in common with the grass
that lives, but briefly lives as flesh that sings within their summers, flesh

that is bestowed on them and they in turn pass on, giving up
their temporalities. How can they live as flesh when that flesh
that soars is all that they, suspended in the sun, inhabit, its
falling inexorably away—but birds remain, their songs still
ascendant, flesh transposed, the emptiness that stands around them heard,
the flesh thrown open, its invisibility a strophe that
is our incarnate turning with the sun, our possession air?

SUN

We stretched our hands into the air and thought we touched the light, the sun
departing on our hands, a ceremony that displaced us for
the moment from the earth, and we alone were bearing up the sun,
the cries of dying generations nowhere in our ears, nor was
there any there for us to see, the light that fell upon our hands
the one fall, the things of its illumination unremembered,
nothing standing up inside our minds and taking shape without

a thought. We are eclipsed, a moon of absolute cessation, no
opacity between us and the sun. It was not possible
to think that this was primal or an ending—: it was light
in all that it could be as light, and we were light, the touch of its
descent the touch that makes of us the sun. In us the world wakes,
no element that is not in the fire, nothing, stone or tree,
the thing they are another sun we thought was shade within the light.

SUNSET

I look at you across a field of long remembered trees. The sun
is setting in your hair, and you are but a schema standing up
against the sky where birds in their minute nocturnal gatherings
would disappear, translated into that appearance that you make.
The time that rises up between us, drifting through the branches, is
a sleeping bird, the silence of its breathing all that we can hear
within the field, the words of our conversation what it says.
The time that trees would keep is ours in this minute, not the time

of suns returning—: time for us stands up and opens, plenitudes
of air the history they know, and in the air a memory
of other trees exchanged where we recall ourselves, the ground a bare
fermata where the we that we would be arises, our air
an air remembered, trees that sing their slowly cadenced paeans of
the sun's descent into their bodies, keeping time as what they are,
their rising up to be the sun incarnate, heavens their release
of breath, and ours in the now arboreal of setting suns.

RENAISSANCE

All my bones I give to you, the bones that I received when I
was born, and yours you give to me, and so we are, born again,
the rib that you possessed the rib that now is mine, an Adam and
an Eve complete, anatomies that are exchanged, a sun and moon
that are in mutual eclipse, the light between them light that is
not of the sun but both. What is it that within this garden leaps
into the air where apples are not apples but the light that falls
across the sun and moon, and what are all the bones that we were sure

were our shapes in their divided solitudes? They are bones
of what we thought we were, possessed of their propriety,
the sun upon their skins, the moon revolving in the darkness of
the mind apart. The bones were bones, and we were pantomimes, the bones
in us the props that made us shadows, wind, and grass, the things that we
have left in little heaps of time, alone and turning back to dust,
but our bones are ours now, not yours or mine, the moon and sun
a stone dissolved in fire, orchards apples dancing on our hands.

EMILY

All that veiled your body from the world was your dress, a cloth
of purity and death. It owns your vacant room, standing in front
of us in its translucent cage, and you inside it all–the glass,
the vacuumed air, the emptiness within, where God and sparrows, seas
and absence all consorted with each other, ecstasy and grief
synonymous within your purity and death which you put on
to dress the page before us with one stroke, inarticulate

and bare, its gesture toward eternities of glass where suns in their
abstractions fill the air in one perpetual fall, a stroke so grave
and careless none could think that it could end, of flowers stroked and grass
that every year returned. Your dress endures, its purity and death
hermetically contained. What is this cover of your flesh
that we should think that it prevails? To dust it will return, the glass
and God together blown into the nothing where beginning is,

the endless blank where you have gone, a single stroke and all erased,
and there you are, the pure potentia of gesture in the air
invisible that no reliquiae can grasp. Eternities
stand up within the air around us all and dressed in shapes of no
colour to see, each an alphabet that does not speak but breathes
the breath of verbs in their initial purity, of verbs undressed,
the one adornment an ekstasis of the stricken sun, the light

a universe laid bare, an a priori of the dust, the air
the only visible to know, and there, in that verb where you
no longer know but are, the air itself begins, the ictus of
the that of that which is, the other side of God and grass, the air
that falls forever through the emptiness of air, the moving sun
but dust, but dust that moves in musicalities that are the are
of an inflection where hiatus halts–a book of open hands.

O

Certain things are noticed first: the colour of the sky is of
a colour that has stopped beside the clouds that are unmoving on
a colour that resembles palest blue, the trees have opened to
the limits of their most inspirited largesse, the light suffused
from somewhere that remains unbidden by the sun, and every house
is standing in the place of its original foundation full
of light, reflecting clouds, the unbelievable resemblance of
the sky. A clock has struck, the echo of its music hovers in

the air and takes upon itself a colour of the sky that is
incapable of being other than its first expanse of blue,
an echo, then, of blue that falls again upon our faces that
appear to be another music filling space until the end
of music high against the sky from where it falls again, a rain
of distance and of blue, and all there is to hear within the air
is o and o and o that fills the country of our childhoods
with inarticulate, precise refrain. Our faces are no more

than this, each a round and periphrastic turn of blue, and there,
inside, roses stand, one a mirror of the other, receding
toward the farthest sky of roses echoing with roses. We
are innocence that strays unknowing into its incapable
and barely speaking o—or mirrors of a light that is of no
departure, light that only is and in its lightness places us
alone in our self-reflection, compasses of our where
that measures our replies that in our eyes is but roses and their o.

GARDENS

The smallest flowers tumble from your mouth, taking places in
the air at random, roots invisible but spreading everywhere
among the planets of their own conception, flowers passing through,
the where of their beginnings nowhere but approximate, beside
themselves for instants, then departed, music flagrantly surprised,
a silent laughter rising from the flesh exposed to rains that fall
from stars that have gone out already one by one, a music of

no signature than that of its devising, temporalites
that fall without direction through each other, flowers brushing up
on their surprising flowerness, falling open into words,
the fountain of your mouth falling empty into the emptiness
of air where words stand up beside you and themselves in flower, air
the only terra firma of their being, Primavera's mouth
that smiles on the fallen autumns of the world, benevolence

that gathers what is left of 'opposites collapsing,' finitudes
of whatever is, its joy and sorrow, simple nuances of
forgotten afternoons no longer in your hands, but afternoons
that are in flower instantly, at random here and there and gone,
Primavera's smile disappearing into words and then
the airs of memory, the air of its blessure and blessing, spring
of all that is washed up to flower *sponte sua* upon your breath.

LATER

When the gods were known to have been somewhere in the world, they
were seen as sudden changes in the air, the sun displaced for what
seemed hours in the ancient sky as they would pass alone or in
procession, planets pausing and the moon, no longer stone, awake
with light, the space around it charged with colours never known to break
from prisms found upon the ground, and after they were gone, they would
remain in mind as colours no one could describe, the similes

unravelling and spilling useless in the air, the nearest that
could be attempted was to speak of flowers, small flowers in their
retreats where only wary climbers find them grasping when the risks
are greatest, climbers coming back with eyes that are incapable
of seeing anything but those remembered colours, traces of
the gods in their approximations still alive and standing in
their eyes, a world where divinity is but a memory

of something nearly blue, nearly as the sky is seen, a sky
almost, remotely blue, the nearest blue that we can hold within
our eyes, and holding it possessing what of gods is left, the earth
awake in us in its primality, no other way for it
to know itself as earth but in the moment of the passing of
the gods in us, the light unnameable, impossible to hold
the earth, its knowledge, its deliverance of itself in us recalled.

TURN

Coming into town, that road came from somewhere in the past.
All the fields around it had been cleared, and one tree beside
it had been spared, the crown of its surviving spreading shade across
the road and fields where wagons slowly came overflowing with
the harvests, horses straining forward with their burdens, measuring
their pace with hidden stars, their rhythms rhythms in the cadence of
stories that were chanted under younger stars where gods and nymphs

were known to pass barely noticed, stories that were not made to end
but dilate, measured stories turning in a dance of stars that spoke
and disappeared until their turn came round again, the causes of
their movements unexplained but seated in their motions through the air.
The wagons that we saw, the horses and the tree, were what we saw
and something that we heard as we might hear the stars we could not see
that once were stars that saw the gods at play, the dancing nymphs, the words

that once spoken flower in the fields beside the roads, no
beginnings but the ground from which they rise, a singing fire of
their movement through the seasons, no conclusions but to flower as
other flowers open in the words of our stories passed between
us through the harvests of our nights, each a choreography
that has its shape fulfilled as word and star, the measure of
the dance the place of what we are, its gravity its turn in us.

ROSARIA

Roses speak, their speech an infinitesimal unfolding of
the slowest time, of time remembered in its actualities,
known before, but stored as bees might be in an infinity
of amber, wombs where worlds wait to be, articulations of
desire and its logos. Speaking rose! the farthest stone upon
the farthest moon finds its echo in your mouth, its silences
at first unutterable given voice. So roses, then, if stones

in their unageing stay within their mouths, archival stones that are
of time the deepest recollection, roses stand about us our
cosmos where the moons and sun must be the fullness of their times
expressed, and we are what is spoken to them our speaking a
reply, the realization of the rose that now in us becomes
the music of itself, the moon a modulation of the moon,
its desire floating into time upon our tongues, the moon

and sun and smallest stones now leaping up, rosarias of speech
that play within our mouths. We have no other voice than what we are
given to remember, time beginning in the sun that in
its rising rises now in us, all the knowing stones have held
given up to be the mind of roses turning in the fire,
pentecostal on our tongues, infinities the moment that
the stone in us possesses, tempos of roses speaking rose.

ANATOMIES

I did not know my bones until I knew of yours that in my hands
have grown so in their familiarity that they are in
my body bearing something of your shape and mine together, a
revision of what I had thought I was, a vision of a flesh
that is not seen but known, and what we are a lake where fish unknown
flow in from rivers where our shores are open, willows sending roots
along the memories of an outside, a lake that only seems

to be itself, a lake that is of water that would settle through it for
a season, lake that has no colour that it does not borrow as
the light allows, a lake of nothing that it claims its own but what
it knows as pieces of its composition, the you and I of our
random motions somewhere else, of things that were but were
where nowhere comes and goes, impossible to bring to mind, the sky
that rests upon us through the night a sky where stars lie down upon

us lightly where we meet the air, stars that in their polar arcs
are then so near to us that we are sure that they are our breath,
constellations taking temporary residence in us,
anatomies that are beyond our will to shift, an orient
that is of what we are, possessed of largest latitudes where rain
descends among the stars and through our flesh, the mind that moves in us
a ritual of galaxies, its gestures prayers in our hands.

TOWNS

All the towns of our childhoods are now arrested in
that other now of their eternal sabbaths, mirroring themselves
but resting in an absence unassailable, the symmetry
of trees upright along the boulevards, the sun suspended in
the afternoons of long forevers, people on the street about
to lift their feet and move, a dog that starts to bark, the sound unseen
against horizons of the stars in other constellations: why
are they the only towns where we meet and under stars that have

no names for us, the we we meet uncovered always but for those
stars whose light pours down upon our bodies as a rain that falls
through dreams of rain, unable to translate the we that our eyes
gaze upon? Showers of stars are what our bodies are that rain
upon the smallest towns in their eternal pauses, falling through
their silhouettes dimly cut out against the darkness. Roses rise
invisible in us, the light the shape of their becoming rose,
almost opening, the stars upon us barely touching ground.

BREVITY

Everything we know is open in the rose that stands here
between us, the petals that we think it is enfolded on the core
of its indwelling in itself, the earth that rises in it and
the sun alchemical upon the gesture of its place between
our hands, a movement that we hold, its knowledge resident in what
is here, but knowledge open and without conclusion, nothing then
to grasp, a nothing that with our knowledge of its brevity

overflows, but flows over into the air that sheathes our hands,
our brevity the rose we hold, its knowledge and the open of
its giving in to us, and what was ours given back, the earth
in us and sun, not we but transmutations of the rose, the light
that falls across us where we live, the night and day departed, air
our only country and the breath of roses rising over us,
our hands the transience of birds invisible within our eyes.

AUTUMNAL

Deeper into the autumn woods we walked, beneath the trees that shed
silence on our bodies moving over the late summer smell
of grass, the rain that fell during the night. The animals that walked
somewhere near were moving through their distances, the trees around
them casting silence, all of us drawn into that enfolding fall,
the trees alone appearing not to move unless the silence that
expanded from their breathing was the motion that was moving us,
animals invisible, the stars that are within their skies,

the air growing larger in our eyes. Deeper into autumn
we walked as one, the silence that was falling resting on our flesh
to be what we would see when we would turn to look upon the trees
that seemed to change beneath the light, somewhere in the sun brightness
standing in our eyes, resplendent, silent opening of fall
that lies upon us where the animals that move in our sphere
disappear, their exits a diminishment of light among
the trees. Deeper we walk, our pace the pace of animals that have

walked into us, their lairs the silence that envelopes us, and we
are of the trees, but trees that move upon the grass, our breath of one
exhalation of the silence that is our shape. There are
no words that fall upon our tongues, but were we moved to speak, the light
that leaps upon the trees would dance upon our tongues, its rhythm not
a movement known to us, of stars we cannot see, animals
whose distances are our bodies in their deepest fall, and we
are silence that, when it speaks, utters autumn, sounds of falling stars.

FLOWERS

You placed flowers in a bowl, the end of summer floating on
the water, each flower an emblem of every flower that
had stood before them through the other summers of their brief lives
and deaths, and floating in a bowl it is the eye of summer that
we see, its gaze in its dispersal, the minutiae of space
within its small circumference, the moon suspended in its course,
its light swelling among them, light and memories of night, the breath

of summer's exhalation floating upward in the room around
us, taking us within its breath, and we are now but seasons, you
and I, their transience the aura of eternity that is
our one possession, flowers, then, of flowers that are of a time
where time is in its fullest flower, open and contained within
the gaze of its unending overflowing: we are summer, its
gift at rest within our hands, the shape we are the blown moon.

HORIZONS

We passed a place where all the houses and the store were on our left,
facing south upon command, it seemed, across an emptiness
that rose upon our right and stood there summoned by the presence of
that brief collection of the houses and the store. The sun did not
move, it burned against the glass of several windows, and we saw
it was the silence of the glass that was on fire, all the houses
closed to sight. It was to enter fire, an emptiness consumed,

and as we moved, and as the emptiness that was the place in its
completion disappeared, we saw that we were of the fire, no
distance anywhere, the sun and its reflections our place,
to be inside an azimuth, the polar of its origin
the space our bodies were. We cannot tell if our moving or
the fire in its turning is the infinite of passage, the sun
where we become horizons of each other's where, our breath the light.

ANGELS

Angels lay before us in the snow, angels unadorned and in
a shape that made them seem to be of us, but us in likeness of
something we might possibly have been where other suns had once
passed by, shaped by shadows left to be inferred, but shadows that
were not of us but angels, prostrate and unable to return
our gaze. This is where we were, alive upon the snow, the air
of winter settled over us. We knelt to touch what we had done,

to grasp our heads in purest outline pressed against the sun, our arms
that had become what we believed were wings, and finally all of us
were known by our hands, but barely, touching what we are as we
become our memory. The shadows of the afternoon within
us there are blue, impossible to touch. Even the snow inert
upon the ground that memorizes us possesses movements of
the sun, the wings that we have risen from are stirred by currents of

an air that falls invisible inside the snow, another time
inhabiting our shades, assuming seasons on their empty shapes,
our memories ascetic but abandoned to the shifts of snow
where flowers will, and birds and unaccustomed summers, rise upon
the shapes of our memories, the custom that we keep the turn
of what we cannot see, the we of what we were a place where snow
falls, our origin of angels, flowers open in their shade.

THAT

Before the first thought of worlds, of times to filter through the seas
and airs, the smallest mollusk somewhere in its cosmos, before the first
tree began to open on the lips of where it first was heard,
the that of everywhere was silence, gods unformed, and breath about
to be, and if within the silence something fell, its fall would have
no echo anywhere, but everything that was to be was in
the silence that it carried forth when it began, a motherhood
of silence, the sign of its passing through the world given it,

the bones of our anatomy that do not speak to us but are
of memory the greater shape, and not of us but of that that
of us when we unspoken stood among the virtualities
of worlds, the o of no measure that is ours that, when we
within the silence of our bodies know, restores in us the shape
of roses, seas, the careless birds before they were as now they are,
our silence that recursive ecstasy that is the now
of that now before before was thought, our bones the that unsaid.

WHERE

Of all mortalities, words are first to leave us, borne aloft
upon the evening air, the fireflies of our voices, and,
no sooner gone, begin to dance with light that we had not perceived
before, a light of their volition where the air before our eyes
begins to change, and what we spoke from our lips, the we that says
we is now among the trees and grass, occasions of a thought
that we had not considered, fragilities of words unburdened of
our breath and our desire are of evening, light, and dance without

a choreography that is known to us, making of us
the where of their departure into dark, a destiny that we
had not determined, but a we in our translation, given us
to see, mortalities that are of no conclusion, the we of what
we make a thing that taking us escapes us, the there of our there
no longer where we say we are but somewhere in the evening that
descends across our flesh, the evening where the trees, the late light
upon their branches, stand, the evening filled with our ignited breath.

DOMA

We gathered up the little lakes and took them home—the fish that sleep
beneath their surfaces, the trees along the shores that shelter them,
the birds that cast their sudden shadows on the water—lakes and their
environments were placed in our house, and we would sit within
their seasons, floors beneath us but of grass, and where the ceilings were
the skies of several lakes arose, the air more various: we lived
with them and they with us until it was that we became for them

their seasons in their passage, autumns radiant in their conclusions,
snow and rain we were, a moon that finds its light dispersed upon
the water through the longest nights, at one with stars that see themselves
afloat in us and on the lakes. And so we are a knowing that is
not seen with our eyes but visible within our bodies, nor
is it given other than as parable that writes itself
in that place where air in gusts moves past, the colour of the lakes

now this, now that, and you might say that all of it—the we as we
would think we were, the water, air and changes in the light—was on
the point of speaking, and if they did, to speak in tongues not their own,
and we would speak as water, lakes would murmur with the chant of rain
upon their faces, rain itself and sun in our mouths as our
words, all of us an analogue of all that is, and where
we thought the centre was is there, at home upon the shores of lakes.

APPEAL

The voices floating up toward us aloft within the evening air
seemed ours, voices lifting above the grass and up toward the trees
to pause suspended in the air and what there was to see, but they
could not be seen, and how we hoped that they were stars that had leaped forth
directly from the hands of God to fill the evening air with light
that was unending in its moving through the dark, stars that had
no constellation but that changed the order of the cosmos, each

another sound our voices took against the silence everywhere
as they come back to us from that divinity of what we spoke
in darkness and the absence of the light. If we are to know
ourselves and where we come from when we speak, we have no more than this—
nothing to see but memories of stars and how they might begin,
the ghosts of trees and grass where we remember how we might have heard
ourselves, had we been there, appealing to each other in the night.

SNOWING

When snow comes, it comes from everywhere at once, no single point
sufficient to explain the way it comes and goes, a whiteness that
explodes, the landscape where it is a place of stillness absolute,
not dead but things that are unable where it is: it seems as if
not one but all eternities are breaking open in the snow
and no before or after can be possible, the only time
the snow, and it a time that cannot be comprised. How do we find

ourselves here, every centre multiple and passing on
the wind? To speak is hardest, words torn up around us, the snow not snow
but etymologies of snow, the syllables enough and each
conjoining momentarily with each, the babel of our speech
another snow, another passage. Here we stand up, you
and I invisible but heard, a snow of raging birds, their cries
fragments of the fallen skies upon our breath becoming white.

BODIES

All that we are given is the bodies where we are, and when
we look, the distance that extends between us and the grass is as
immeasurable as the space that opens in the mind where stars
revolve and disappear, their passage in us endlessly, the space
they make an overture of flesh and bone. I have seen you be
my afternoon, the light that grows leaner across the snow and past
the trees is light that is in you, the shadows of it rising from

your face, unfathomable shadows that have come from where you have
descended, shadows that cannot be read, but shadows that are of
your body, steeped in distances that fill your flesh. What are they if
not you, embodying that space, a memory invisible
that moves between us, our knowledge of it knowledge of
our flesh that touches it and hands it back and forth, unknowing what
it does, but in us shadows settle, afternoons, and in our bones

the light that made them dances in infinities of other light,
our bodies turning in the light, their knowing knowing of it as
the time they keep, of bodies that continually come and go
through the light and into dark, their temporalities the place
where knowing disappears and in its stead the light that is in us
is what we are, as trees where light lingers as leaf and then distills
itself into itself. We are the afternoon, the shade, the sun.

IF you were moved to speak these words, my request would be for you

to say them *maestóso*, face upon the ground, your hair a shroud
that puts the sun out, the stars forever buried somewhere in
the ground and in a room like this one where we have arrived at last,
its space composed of silence, shreds of dark, where overhead there are
pillars that support the nothing of the air: the trees have never
thought to grow upon this ground, and in the blank vacuities
of air nowhere are there birds or sounds of living things. We walk

into the earth, beneath the pillars and the place where you have left
the shape your face lay down. Around us nothing but the dark, and in
the dark the light of candles rises up, their light alone perceived,
and it is everywhere, a light of fireflies without the sense
of anything inside but darkness that the light surrounds, a piece
of all the dark that falls into the ground, falling with the pace
of floating stars, and in the air impossible to see the names

of all the children who have died, their names the spoken shape of this
eternity that opens up around us, an eternity
of darkness flowering, the night itself in flower, black and full
of memories of fire passing through the frailty of bones,
the little bodies blown to ash that rise and fall before our eyes,
eternities of ash that are no more than leaves that disappear
into the autumns of a silence infinite and bare. Perhaps

their immortality is where we are, walking slowly through
the gyre of their being that cannot be seen, but opens in
the space between each name, and we cannot go anywhere, and so
we stand inside the silence that their names inscribe upon the air,
every child an infinity of children that goes out
into the universe to be the stars, the cosmic dust, no more
these children but millennia of children that rise up in us

becoming our breath, a circulation in the words that we
might speak but are unable, speaking only silence, ash,
and light that is not light but light in memory suspended on
our tongues where they are who they are immortal, the only immortality
that they possess the shape of dancing that is all around us in
the air beneath the ground, of little bones that leap as fire leaps,
the dancing space that they have entered space where our bodies are:

we are the absence here, and they the cosmos playing over us,
the motion of the stars the what of what they are, invisible
but ours as a gravity that is incapable of being
held within our hands, a gravity of fire that is in
them, the eternity that is the dark in flower, flowering
for us, its silence all that we are given stretching forth into
the ground, the nothing that we are dispersed into their going past.

Yad Vashem, Jerusalem

ENTRANCE

You heard a music we could not, and entering the room, you turned
to leap into the air, and when you left, no one said that they
had seen what you had done, but everyone had seen, and what they saw
was not the sunlight in your hair, but where the sun had shone, and where
it was was where your hair had been, another sun, your hair a fire
that was of a fire we had never seen, and when it came
into our memory, we had no word for it or for the dance
that it became, but all about us light came down upon our flesh,

and if it had been rain, we would have seen ourselves as figures in
a sudden shower, falling without any motion of the wind,
a rain that came and just as soon was gone, the rain another skin
for us, to take our shape and hold us so in its forgiveness, all
of us invisible within the light, the dance that it would make
the dance that was of you and of what was invisible but on
our flesh that leapt when you rose up into the air, its emptiness
transfiguring our memories into a music of the light,

the rain that did not rain, eclipsing what had been within us as
the shape of what we thought we were, a fire that was purely fire
without the ash of something left behind to say that it was fire
we had seen, and so it was not possible to say what we
had seen, no longer what we thought what we had been, becoming what
fire is when fire is the place where we begin, the sun
the dawn and dusk at every moment now in us, the room a sign
of space that fills itself, a universe that leans against our hands.

NOCTURNAL

Your mouth opened, and in your mouth the night arose, and there we found
ourselves within the dark. A tree stood up within the night, and in
the tree we saw a bird upon a branch, a little bird that now
and then would hop onto another branch and stop to stare into
the night. If you had spoken then, you would not have been capable
of saying words, but out into the world from your mouth the night
would have begun to spread, a tree would have been seen against the sky
in darker lines, and then a little bird would have set forth to hop

into the space that you had nearly uttered, a bird that if there were
a moon would have appeared illumined as he hopped, the light around
him everywhere, his feathers throwing light into the air, and it
would seem a little burst of snowy light that played within the tree,
but not a sound was heard except of breath, and when you breathed, the night
in motion settled instantly upon our skin, a night that felt so light
it seemed a passing bird, a bird without a song, unless the moon
sang, and near us branches breathing, answering in silence yours.

TRANSIENCE

Nothing seems so transient as that light that rests upon
the sea, a slow, undulant expansion of the light that is
not the moon alone and not the stars, but their diffusion through
the air until it is uncertain where the light, dancing across
the infinite of water, finally comes from—: our eyes
are filled with light, through our eyes the sea comes in, and we are its
horizons, tides in their refluxions what we know of breath, the light
returned. The world we inhabit is without hypothesis,

the brevity of light the brevity that is how we appear.
I do not see you anywhere but in my eyes where seas extend,
the moon behind you with the farther reach of stars, and you are not
a moment in its sheath of flesh but of the undulations that
is water dancing through the slowest nights, the sky fallen upon
your shoulders. The time the moon keeps is ours, its departures the
invisible that is the breath exhaled when moon and breath lie down
together on the shores of our sea, their contours indistinct,

and we are overflowing with the disappearance of the cosmos
we believe is ours, the moon gone, the emptied sky, the night the one
reflection of our mind bereft of light, but nowhere is the moon
but in the sky of our breath, its undulations ours. We
do not know—no more than the moon—incapable of any sure
containment of the passing light, the sea in us and everywhere,
the motion of its tides a conversation holding us, and our
silence, its turning turning on our tongues, a meaning drifting past.

INTERMEZZO

At night, when layers of the dark enfold us, you begin to sing,
your voice emerging from the nowhere of your sleep, the curve of its
crescendos floating over us until we are drawn into it,
the darkness and the music our element, the sound it makes
a music from the bottom of a well, a music, then, that rises
from the deepest pools of water, water that is sunk into
an age of things before the mere arrival of the rain, before
what we would summon up as breath upon the waters brooding, a

refrain it is without the interplay of words where memories of
something that had been before the rise of firmaments when we
could not have been, a dark composed of music known alone to all
the dark, the only all, and from it us and water and the air,
and through it music that sojourns in you and then unbearably
arises, taking us into whatever was before there was
what we might think could be, the darkness and its music all that we
possess, and it possessing us, the music ours and the dark.

PIGEONS

Your eyes are rain, another rain but rain that drifts slowly over
us, and we belong to it, its unforseen retreats and quick
returns, and in the rain we heard the calls that pigeons make to one
another, music welling up with cadences that follow where
the rain desires, music that is in repose and deep inside
it, calling to itself of its perfection, never heard so well
but in the rain, both rain and music, something that is neither rain

nor music but the way your eyes transpose themselves in certain lights
that take them unaware, and we are held outside of time, possessed
by light and by its passage in your flesh, no other soul inside
you but this—light that rises in your eyes and overflows into
the air, its lightness no more visible than music drifting through
the rain, but in your eyes a music stays that we can neither see
nor hear, and through the soundless nights where we lie down, music falls.

GAZING

A flower stood before us open in the light, a flower that
was nothing more than what it was, its colour tangible, the sun
abandoned there, and our hands were quiet, no desire to
approach it but to leave this open shaping of the summer where
it was, too fragile for our touch, unwilling to possess the light
where it had paused. Knowledge of finalities was not what drew
us here, unwilling to believe that flowers, light or summers open could

give up a secret more than we could grasp, but they must know what we
cannot, to be through summer after summer passages of red
and blue where suns go down at night and disappear, to be the place
where light is in its genesis. They are not ours anymore
than music might be ours, certain knowledge of the sun's desires
not revealed, but given as a book that has no words and placed
before us open for a little while and then taken away.

ALL

This is all that we will leave behind—a line of words and at
the end a little silence, then another word that someone else
might speak, and speaking speak the only thing that I have given you,
and folded in it words that you have given back, this long duet
that is the you and I that we become, a tree that flowers where
we used to stand, and after flowers apples that begin to fill
the air with autumn light, a tree that is a dream of apples where

the light that fills our eyes when we are in each other's gaze is that
refulgence that becomes an apple through the turning year, a sun
that hangs so lightly on the branch that just the merest breath might carry
it away, the breath the words that cast us up in one embrace,
words that made of us the sun and apples and autumnal airs—
these are all I had for you, the little world where we are
but are another self that is not ours, asleep inside the light.

TREES

We thought we saw the trees that stood upon the ground, but what we saw
was what there was left over from the mystery that was beneath
the ground, an afterthought of what we could not see, and in them birds
asleep, the sun in leaf, and we lay down beneath them, closer to
the ground where grass came up against our skin. We pressed our ears as near
as we might come to earth and darkness filled us, overflowing from
us everywhere, and when we looked upon the ground, silence lay

beside us, full of light, the sun asleep inside it: we were in
the sun, our bodies flowing with the light, the leaves that were above
us moving on our flesh in shadows that became for us all
the clothes that we could bear. I saw you then, the only way you are,
the sun appearing here and there among the leaves, and we began
to move as silence moved, our gestures with the pace of music that
is heard as we might hear a shadow in the silence of the sun,

a music that can only be inferred from how the silence comes
and goes, and that was our silence that had made us seem as if
we were a pair of bodies dancing in the light, but bodies that were moved
by silence that had taken us in hand, and when it did, the dance
was one that silence made, and we were silence visible beside
the trees that are the place where we are known, and our dance a dream
that they possess and given over to the sleeping birds to sing.

BELLS

The only time we live is now, the moment when the sun withdraws
and shadows move across your face, a moment that does not appear
to have beginning but was with you from a time when time alone
was all there was, a clean eternity that rests upon our tongues—:
if we are anywhere at all, it is beside the sea, a sea
invisible within the shade, and bells are ringing over it,
the sound of music falling on our bodies filled with water and

the memories of other seas suspended in it, water music
welling up in shade, a cloth that does not cover us but plays
upon our flesh, upon the sand and sea, the body of the earth,
a body we cannot discern as other than our own, the shade
upon your face a shade of music. Gravity is where we touch
our bodies, but the moment when we touch is in the tempo of
a sea of music flowing over us, the air, the shores, the bells.

EPOCHE

The flowers growing on the fence are so heavy with their fragrance
you would think that they must fall at any moment and lie down
upon the ground, and in their falling each say *o*, the syllables
that they become playing in the air, the breath that they exhale
a change of light, the sun in smaller sighs about to set. You might
have said that they, the long exhausted afternoons of their unfolding,
were a sealing of the air with their mortality that was

put forth for us to touch, to feel closure and its passage there
where our flesh was, but what I heard was not your words, it was
another *o* of your reply, the colour of your breath a part
of everything to hear, the flower of your open mouth turned up
and close upon the falling sun. If we are time made visible,
what is the music held suspended here, the light about to fall
where nothing moves but our breathing of the flowers going round?

WORD

The word we wanted most we found upon the ground, and nothing else
was next to it, but just the air that lay upon it and on us.
We could not tell what letters made it up, nor from what book of words
it might have fallen there, and after an eternity of evenings
where the only world given us to know was what we knew
upon our fingertips, we saw beside it shapes of what appeared
to be the stars that rose and set around the word, the table and
the darkness of our bodies standing in the room. The stars were not

like any stars that we had known, but stars that were to be the stars
that stand around our world, and the dark that we had been
the stillness where their light comes from. The stars we know are moments of
a light beginning in the night of their possession, nights that are
another language we cannot set forth alone, its letters stars
that put together what we know without our knowing what it is
we know besides the burning of their light in our flesh where they
spell out desires of what we desire, our bodies stars.

POEM

We are talking in the dark before we fall asleep: it is
not always certain what we say, but flowers flower in the night
beside us, something of the past before the past we hold as ours
rises up among them, places one of us has never seen
exactly as they were, a smell that has completely disappeared,
the look in someone's eye that has gone out—all of this drifts past
us in the dark to come again in dreams, the flowers of our words
anthologies that are composed of us when we are side by side

in silence, knowledge of us our breath alone that rises in
the night invisible—yet all that we have said is not within our grasp,
the words that float upon our voices flowers that are flowers for
themselves alone, and we do nothing more than give them birth, bearing
witness to a shape that gathers form and meets another shape,
the two transformed forever, leaping from our mouths to dance away
into the dark, the darkness changing with their passage through the air
that is a fall into another sleep and dream that come from us

but not from one of us alone, and so we are, but what we are
is not as it appears, a word that follows other words, but words
that are what we become in unforeseen analogy, the words
that are for us the memory we have of us without recall that take
us as we are—the voices of our bodies, their inflections, signs
of their mortality—into their grasp, the little that we know
in our darkness now in flower, what we could not do now done,
our flowers knowing us for us, to keep us in our sleep.

ROOM

You were sitting on the floor: familiarities of chairs,
remembered tables where they always were, your hands raised up to hold
the air, solitude at rest upon your flesh. The darkness in
the room was all there was of time, of time that came and settled there,
its homeliness a night that finds its way in us invisible
but something you might touch, a dust of darkness passing over all
of us that stays behind when we imagine it is day, the dark
dispelled. But this was darkness absolute, the shape your hands took

unable to be seen where in them darkness opened, a small star
in flower there, a focus of the universe that fell asleep upon
your open hand at home. We might have asked what it might be if we
had words upon our tongues, but silence filled our bodies, falling through
the space of where our room had been, a light too large for what we held
of knowledge and its shapes, its radiance our only place, and what
it was what it would say—not star, not light, but something that we could
not grasp but given up, a thing that only darkness brings and takes

away, and in its substance kin to our breathing, punctual
forever in our flesh, a brilliance that has no horizon but
beneath the fall of darkness resident in us. So we, if there
were anything for us to see, would know that we are where there is
no end of us in sight, the farthest flower that is open in
what is for us invisible is in the light that is in us,
the breath we cannot see its breath around us in the dark, the walls
that we had known unknown, and our room the dark in flower there.

DREAM

Your voice when you wake up is full of dreams that linger as a child
might before departing, hesitant upon the sill, abandoning
his mother's house to disappear into the light of day, never
to return except in memory at home in solitudes,
but gradually the name and then the face forgotten, nothing to
remind us that it had been here before it went away, the only
trace the way your voice takes flight within the twilight of our room,
a voice divided from itself that hovers everywhere within

the air in fragments calling to themselves in their dispersal, not
as one but many voices lost, polyphonies of stars, but stars
gone out, and their departure the removal of a universe,
no polar space in sight to grasp familiarity, the room
a bare collapse of air, and we unable in the rising light to know
what we we might have been, enveloped by a silence that is not
of music in suspension, but a silence of eternal absence,
our bodies now no more than light that falls thoughtless through our hands.

TIME

Time lay down upon the ground and slept, genesis itself
enfolded in the grass. We stood upon our toes to walk around
it, fearing that our slightest gesture might awaken it. We did
not notice right away that something in the sun had changed, and light
that fell upon us fell from everywhere, the sky become the sun,
and where there had been planets, moon and stars was but the cleanest light
that we had yet beheld, and when I saw you standing there, it was
not possible to grasp the you I knew but you in palimpsest
beneath the light was all I saw, where you were written once before

as I had known you when the time that now lies down was where you drew
the shape I barely see, and in the light your body moves against
the edge of time, your body speaking breathlessly to mine, and both
of them begin to move together, knowledge moving back and forth,
and nothing to be heard, a naked light exchanged and passing through
a twinkling of an eye: eternity can last no longer, its
calligraphies the only shape that's visible inside the light,
the earth unfolding from the grass and flowing back into the sky,
and there the silence speaks, an empyrean etched upon our hands.

MORNING

We spoke of where, when we have passed beyond this life, our life might be,
if we will be again, and where it was did not appear as we
have read in books, a place of certain majesty where all the dead
are standing cloaked in their serenity, the sun upon them always
and the sound of singing that is not like any singing we
have heard. It is not so, was what you said, it is a little house,
and all the life that follows this is in it in a corner, nowhere

else, and we are in the house that holds the one forever that
there is for us. Windows are there where morning is the only light
that falls. It is the house where all there is is light, and when we wish
to sleep in our eternity, we lie upon the light, and when
we speak, it is the light that speaks, a naked light that is what we,
when we were in the other life, became without our knowing, stars
awake upon our fingers. What is there to touch, when we are held

together, hands upon our bodies, fresh eternities, the sun
beside us in the air of where we live, no difference that we
can see between the lives we dream and are, that would not have the feel
of light? Eternity is everywhere: tomorrow it will lie
upon our hands, the weight of it no more than our breath upon
our flesh, the same eternity that we possessed when what we held
we thought was simply us, our bones asleep already on the light.

MORNING GLORY

You never had another face, and it was always as it is—
naked to the sun. If it had been a tree, it would have been
a tree that lived wherever summer was, the wind forever lifting
through its leaves, and this would be the face that I have seen, a face
whose only shape was how the wind would open it, and when I thought
I saw your eyes, it was but light that had not entered them before,
a light that fell through tempers of the leaves that moved against the tree

that was your face when it had risen up in me a tree, the sun
inside it and in leaf. But what would be within my hands if they
would take it now? It is not possible to grasp what I have seen,
no more than I might lift the light itself when it had fallen on
the ground, an offering of summer going past, nor grass that stands
where it had fallen and the air where everything that is that is
your face now comes to rest, the moment of it dawning through my eyes.

RECITATIVE

Yours is a voice composed of slow recitatives. The rain could not,
no matter how it falls—hesitant and full of delicate
revisions in the autumn air—approximate the shadows that
return, suspended in your mouth, where night arrives, the moon among
them almost visible, a moon that would be spoken casually
and then forgotten, nothing to be seen but spaces where what you
cannot recall are summoned, silence filling up the shade. The rain does not

possess such silence, silence that when spoken fills us with the slow
assertions that are not your words but what they wear, their shapes as they
descend into the air where they depart, no more remembered than
a moon made up of silence and the shade. This is the music that
is neighborhood for us—a house, a tree, a sky enough above
where silence, flowing from your mouth and into darkness, is the what
of us when we are said, the rain that falls a rain that is our are.

CHILDHOODS

Somewhere my childhood has disappeared into a life that is
its own, and in it stand the unrecoverable trees, the streams
that wandered without purpose underneath them, past the houses that
have gone, the fields that are invisible, a childhood of dimmest
blue that settles over it and yours, the one I have not seen
but is within the shade of mine, a common blue that they assume
in that place of theirs where they reside, their absence ours—not
to be a thing that falls within our sight, but passing through, a gesture

made at random, without the gift of thought, and almost missed. We are
not able then to say whatever it was, and if we saw it, all
of what it was would be the air in movement that becomes a place
of our desire where we stand, and over us a memory
of what is not of me or you, but of a childhood that has
been offered us, rising up from our flesh that is its own
discovery, a world where we beside each other are contained,
to be what we have given to the self we are as we have been.

ECHO

When we awoke, the room where we had slept was full of silence, but
it was such silence that arises after someone speaks, and when
we moved upon our bed to step upon the floor, we saw that it
was not a bed where we were lying but the remnants of what was
before the silence filled us and the room, a word, perhaps, but from
a language we had never heard, a language that would speak and then
depart when we drew near, but in departing leave an echo of
itself where we had been. Nothing was there that we could see—it was

something that hung about our flesh where we had lain, something that we
emerged from in our sleep when we stepped into silence where the air
surrounded us with echos of the speaking dark, its breath still fresh
against us when, the moon upon us and the night, we sleep inside
whatever word it is that holds in our solitude. What are
we then if we are every morning born anew from what is said
in our dark but something that we do not know when we would put
it into words, a place that when the word that holds us opens, speaking

silence from our flesh and breath? The light that lets us see that we
are not the sun and not the room is light that spills from our eyes
and falls on you and me in sudden sense, but sensed as not of us.
If we are meaning, what we mean is meaning for the world—the
returning sun, the tree beyond our window, and the disappearing
moon, impossible for us to say the sentence that embraces
us when we step into silence which is what the world is:
a memory of us that it retains and our origin.

HYPOTHESIS

No one understands what trees say, but echos of their speaking
are on our skin. We think they are the shadows that their leaves lay down,
a little sun around their edges, nothing more. Their echos, then,
are something we suppose, as we suppose the seed beneath the rose,
the seed that disappears into the root, a pure conjecture that
rises in the air that we take in, but when they speak, we are
their antistrophe, our bodies turning back to them to form
whatever sound they make, the syllables of rain that are for us
another flesh, or glimpses of the moon that hides among the leaves
the shape the trees assume. Hypothesis is not a cast of mind,

it is what lies within our hands when our hands are clasping us,
the statements of the possible surrounding us. If we could hear
the last thing the moon would say before it leaves our eyes, its speech
would take a certain shape, the light upon our bodies taking from
them what they have of bodies, prompting them to dance, the music that
they cannot hear a music that is what their bones had been. How else
to answer trees as they upon our flesh invoke us, shades rising
from the moon, its presence we consider stone forgotten in
the air, another body that cannot be seen inside its light?

KNOWING

The little that we know we gathered up together, placing it in
the afternoon, and saw it disappear into the sun, easing
into emptiness, the stars that turn forever at the end
of things invisible around your head, the birds that circle with
them barely heard. It was an emptiness in which another universe
lay down beside us in the dark unnoticed in its moment of
arrival. Protocols were not observed, other austerities
that distance must confer. It was a universe of intimate
pavanes that we mistook as shapes of spring, the trees on holiday,

and we began to find our places in that dance, at first uncertain,
unacquainted with the steps, the long glissades that were not in
our feet but in the air, the quickened ground, the music that we could
not hear: it seemed that we were of the music, its diminuendos
our entry into emptiness, silence that moved through us,
the trees, the stars around your head, without the you and I that we
had thought were who we were. To be arranged so is what we are,
unknowing, no finalities in our movement possible,
a silence open, we are known but known in our turning through—

MOON

A rose grew up inside us unannounced, no one seeing it,
but we were in its knowledge, giving it in our ignorance
the weather where it stands between our bones, a rose that is for us
a place the sun had occupied, and we for it the moon of its
reflection, our solitude an orbit that tells time for us,
but time that is traversed by an eternal sun that has no west
or east, a sun of everywhere that in its midnights hovers on
our bones and their horizons, rose of the invisible. We think

it is a dream, and if we speak of it, we speak as we might speak
of someone met when we were young and seen in moments somewhere on
the edges of the mind, but when we sleep we walk around beneath
its light, certain we are where its light is deepest in the dark,
and stars are our companions, ceremonious and large, our flesh
a passage of the light that falls by chance within us, ours to
regard throughout the night that we are given. We walk with such care—
our bodies not our own, their sense a sphere of light inflecting us.

ALEPH

During the night we touch each other, never taking thought of what
we do, our fingers grazing blindly over our flesh to read
whatever messages there are upon the threshold of the air,
and if we were awake, we might have seen them hovering above
our bodies, an aurora borealis pulsing through the dark.
It is a way of reading dreams, the light that falls into our hands
a dream that seems of our making, dreaming a light that comes upon us
from the larger body of the world where the trees, the trace

of smaller stars, and summers of the dancing bees are speaking in
a tongue that is not ours but becomes the light upon our flesh,
and where in our nocturnal fibrillations we are in the place
of sentences that come and go in silence, something speaking through
us, our bodies a translucent page. And so the trees that rise
within the dream, a greater dream where we are where the dream occurs,
are what we are, the dream in its continual unfolding. It
is not our bodies that we touch, nor light, but passages

of what it is that dreams through us, the dream where our bodies are
the words that they would use, if dreams could speak, and when we touch, we touch
the form of dreams that in their light are dreaming us and how they wish
us to become. The trees were not, nor flowers, moon and rain that falls
into the afternoons, a thing that could be made, but they are of
the dream that dreams through us, its syllables in time: sometimes we
are its uncertainty, a question brought together with a heap
of stars, and sometimes but its breath between the clauses, both exhaled—

there is the sun in its beginnings as the sun, the sun when it
was first imagined sun, innumerable bees on fire yet
to hive, our breath where they become the focus of space, and all
afloat within the breath of God that breathes through ours in our breathing
through the dream, a dream that is not ours but of us, a dream
that dreams itself that we are given to behold as we are dreamt
and in our dreaming are the figures of the dream, the sun as yet
unborn beside us, beginnings of the rain asleep in our hands.

TELLING TIME

You asked what time it was, and I looked up and saw the sun that stood
against the sky. We thought the sun was our time and measure but
forgot to ask the time that was the sun's time, a larger time
than we could see that lay in darkness in the stars, a time of day
perpetual that burns throughout a universe, a time that is
the same forever turning on itself, and in its other times
spiraling out of sight, the time of our childhood inside

it going round, a time when we were young, the sun nothing but
a ball to throw about, time suspended, never knowing we
are for the sun a ball, and when we are, our arms thrown open toward
it, running in its wake, no more than children of the sun we are,
smaller suns that have no other family, the rituals
it keeps a dance that turns minutely on a ground of burning stars,
the place where our bodies light upon a fundament of air.

BIRDS

Birds enough for you and me were sitting in a tree, the night
before its leaving lay upon them everywhere, and songs they might
have made grown still. We looked into the silence that was theirs and ours
which they take to themselves in their invisibility, and when
the light almost appeared, we heard the darkness here and there begin
to open, music falling through the light. We cannot see the light,
it is our seeing, music in it as its measure, all the birds
awake and rising in the air that was the air of what they sang,

the air made visible with birds that might have been a mind, a sea,
an alphabet of falling snow, the birds that sing themselves and in
their song a world visible, but visible as something that
we cannot see before the sun takes note. Silence is the sun
when it is breathing through the dark, and with us in our sleep, the sleep
of dreaming birds our flesh, and from our flesh we are as we arise
for us as we say *you* and *me*: so the sun is spoken, so
a mind of birds that in its early dawn is sung, its silence said.

EVENING

We stepped into the evening, the fullness of it lying on
our shoulders, but without the sense of weight, our feet upon the ground
and not, an evening that was a larger room where stars instead
of chairs were everywhere on hand, their lightness what sustained us. We
did not know how we went our way in silence through the grass, the air
that was around us our only certainty of how a giving
up is to be known, and it was not for us to see yet be
around us everywhere, and all that was for us to see was seen

through it, but more—it is for us a life that we take in in silence,
its invisibility becoming ours. The evening
that we step into is our breath and in our breath the world we
are given to see in its particularity and always one
with us, a gift of air that is the air and our life. If
there was a moment of beginning, an initial breath of air
across the universe, whatever was would have been in its life,
and in a twinkling of eye seen through, its life the life of air,

before it took its shape and place, as stars are shaped and chairs and grass,
a moment when divinity went through them in its fullness, not
for anyone to see but simply to be known by being breath—
the evening where we have stepped, the breath that fills us with
its memory of stars in their eternities. How near we are
to what we are as something that we cannot know, that is but is
for what itself is not, the air that is the one eternity
the fills us with the sense that we and stars are of it for a time—

and see, it does, the trees that stand around us rising up within
our breath, their newest leaves through which the light may still be seen, the moon
behind them but a sliver in the sky, the rest in shade, a moon
that floats upon our breath at home, the ritual of its returns
from darkness ours, another rhythm of our breathing: this is our
eternity, not to be forever as we think we are,
a place where light cannot get through, but what the moon describes when it
departs and then comes back, no more than this, the shape of time gone round.

EYES

When your eyes are closed, the lakes that float across the world close,
the wind falls, and they appear no more but planes of glass that have
no outside for the world, the fish that turn inside them gone from sight,
their gaze upon the deepest of horizons where the dark alone
is visible and shadows are the only substance given—: there
the dark is all that lives, and there your eyes are free to float among
the darkest fish, the trees of stone that grow without the need of light.
Sleep is a waking into dark, the knowledge that it gives a place

where only eyes can touch, as when the moon would touch you on a night
without a moon, its absence radiant in passing on your flesh,
the stoniness that passes through its light passing through your eyes,
and all the stones that lay along the lakes afloat upon the light—
absence, water, and the moon touching in your eyes. The moon
upon the farthest lake appears to rise in sleep, its petals
lying on the surface turned toward the night, a moon that is
a lotus open on the dark, your eyes its night enclosing it.

SUMMER

Where the gate stood open, the smell of flowers came. It seemed that we
had stood beside this fence before—before we knew that we were we,
before we were the children that we were—and all the flowers were
invisible beyond the gate, no more than rapid blurs of colour that
were summer going past, as if it was summer only moving
there, not us, the smell of flowers passing us. We alone
endure, another summer standing up in us, a summer of

hanging fences where the smell of flowers floats serenely on
the summer air, and in them children, children that we were as we
remember them are playing, rising undisturbed by age above
the flowers, gazing at us through the fence with undiscerning eyes,
the way that flowers look toward the sun, their one eternity
in us, a sun for them they cannot see, but flowers that assume
that we are where they are, their summer us, the light we shed

upon them knowledge of their standing near a fence, the twilight and
the sounds of people going by, a town forgotten under trees
that are unknown. A universe could pass, and with it hope, desires
and whatever came to be along the roads and under skies,
but they float up inside us, and alive, the sun we are a light
that is enough to hold them, nothing that they are more moving in
us than the colours that they are, no nearer than the summer air.

TRANSPOSITIONS

The air that moves about us is another skin but closely kin
to ours, a skin of summer light, of apples almost ripe, an air
that has its accents, birds that in their several tongues come over us
so that we cannot say what colour it might be, a dappled air
that sheathes us so we take it for our own, and when we walk, we see
it never leaves us—summer, apples, birds our own—yet moved to speak,
it is another language that we hear that rises in the music

of the birds. Perhaps in paradise no one spoke but sang,
and we were thought to be birds that could not fly, and all we wore,
like them, was sun and moon and stars, and all we said was what we felt
upon our skin and yet transposed, their names unknown, but when we touched,
we brushed against them, summer falling from our mouths however it
had come to be. And so we knew ourselves, our flesh cadenzas of
the rain that moves upon us, sudden moons grown larger in our arms.

TONGUES

A river passed across your face at dusk and disappeared from sight,
but when it passed, it left a moon which lay in fragments dancing on
the water, and beside its banks the grass stood up, a grass you might
have missed beneath the light that was no more than music barely heard,
but when the river passed, you knew the grass that was sister to
the stream, as was the moon, the willows, and the birds that followed it
wherever rivers go in their descents, unfolding out of sight—

and we could hear the echoes of the birds inside their disappearing
music going down, not birds, but memories of birds that live
in us, the birds that are what flesh we are, calling to other birds
that turn careless through the air, the music falling from their mouths
and vanishing from sight. We have gathered this, the longings of
autumnal light that rises up in us to lie upon our breath: we speak
of moons, of nothing else we know, our tongues the stream of their descent.

AGAIN

It seemed the world had departed, and we remained as if there were
an afterthought, standing on the final word of all the final
elegies, a place where suns had been, their setting gone into
ancient time, the shadows of the trees grown larger than the night,
and through the trees we heard the silence of the apples falling—no,
it was an autumn falling, falling through the world that had been,
the air itself too thin to bear our words that fell wherever time

had gone, invisible in autumn light. What stays is something we
had seen, a monk of Zurbarán alone against a wall, and in
his hand a skull that might have held his gaze, and somewhere near a fern
that stood between us and the wall. I wanted all of it—the fern,
the image, and the air that held them there—but what I did not see
was how it is that death befalls one, taking your breath clean away,

all the apples empty to the core, and autumn, and the wake
of falling suns: whatever else, elegy is echo, a light
that is not there, but light that we have seen and so a light that is
invisible, a light that puts the darkness in its place, and through
the darkness an eternity of apples falling deeper into
dusk, and we are echo, not the sound that finally fades away,
but being breathless, breathless autumns, breathless time, again, again.

LEAF

We wanted all the trees to speak as each of them stood naked in
the sudden fall, the light that had erupted through their summer shade
now crumpled at their feet, the silence rising up toward us, a gift
of an infinity to us that opened from the trees into
the farthest light of stars invisible, the silence light that echoed
silence over us, a final leaf that settled on the ground
reverberating all that was unseen around us, our flesh
the farther earth where what they are in their extremities, not flesh

nor season but the rising of a light unknown to us, that
inside of light where we are what is left—of summers, trees and stars—
and our desire that desire that is in the trees as gestures
of mortality in its eternities, and we are not
possessed of anything without this passing of the light, the are
of us a moment of finalities that rises never seen
by us, the breathing that the trees are known to make when theirs is ours,
silences between us never still, and all of us a leaf.